Gallery Books
Editor Peter Fallon

FALLEN

Audrey Molloy

FALLEN

Gallery Books

Fallen
is first published
simultaneously in paperback
and in a clothbound edition
on 1 October 2025.

The Gallery Press
Loughcrew
Oldcastle
County Meath
Ireland

www.gallerypress.com

ISBN 978 1 91737 102 5 *paperback*
978 1 91737 103 2 *clothbound*

A CIP catalogue record for this book
is available from the British Library.

Fallen receives financial assistance
from the Arts Council of Ireland.

the arts council
an chomhairle ealaíon
funding literature

Contents

for the women who wanted more

I am his bride and was and shall be still
tho' infamous as devil's dam, a fear
to wives that watch the cradle side . . .
— Christopher Brennan ('Lilith')

When anyone escapes, my heart
leaps up.
— Sharon Olds ('Stag's Leap')

Fallen

Wives are afraid of me now.
They smile at me the way people smile

at leopards through glass, or across a moat:
how safe we are, over here, in our marriages.

A woman can wake to her own wailing.
How silly, they will say, *this is the sound of guilt*;

think of the children, they'll say, not hearing the plane
at work on her heart, shaving it down to a leaf.

Oh, I read the Russian novels
(and you're not sure now if I mean *read* or *read* —

if this is happening or has already happened.
With loss, both can be true at once).

If the books don't lie I die at the end of the story,
like Anna, or Emma — the fellow-fallen,

how almost *accidental* it sounds! Fallen —
as though I'd lost my footing, stumbled on the lip

of the moat, or slipped like a child's doll
over the glass fence of the enclosure.

What I know of leaving: men stride forth
with purpose, some fine new place in mind.

A wife neither falls nor leaps — she ditches
into the dark hands of the sea,

not caring where she comes to ground,
driven only by what she leaves behind.

The Road Taken

The first time you lie about your heart
you have broken a vow.
You say, I'm taking the dog
for a walk, but you are taking
your heart for a walk
from which it won't return.

I need four hours with you, to explain,
he'd said, and you'd capitulated.
But, Woman, this suburban dog park
is your yellow wood, your roads
diverged, one leading to the horse
latitudes of dinner's-on-the-table,
the other towards the roaring forties.

There's still time to change your mind,
even as he picks his way across the grass
balancing two coffees on a cardboard tray,
even as you spy your little car
parked on the quay; you could fly away home
where your house is NOT YET ON FIRE,
your children STILL THERE.

He looks older from a distance, unsure
and vulnerable, here, midmorning,
his edges soft, like crumbled walls
in the drowned town of your wariness.
Perhaps that's why you don't let go
of the dog's lead, run after her,
run home, keep running.

You are hurtling while standing still.
Hurtling: how it suggests a small hurt —
how tender it sounds as a noun;
how violent as a verb.

His earlier message floats in your mind:
Where are you? I think I am lost.

Early Warnings

FIRST CONTACT

Leonard Cohen's birthday
and the equinox;
something could be afoot.

In your inbox an email: *Dear Mr M____*;
a week later a correction:
Please accept my apology.

He has no idea
you are even a woman
when all this begins.

SWEARING BLIND

Profanity — first thing you like about him;
when he reaches down his throat, hauls up

that shucked red muscle, slides it
across the desk, and you baulk and buckle,

how he swears, all that *effing* and *blinding*,
and how you come around to the unthinkable.

FOOL'S GOLD

He plays you ten songs
from a playlist on his phone.

You listen
politely, searching for clues

to his past loves — his dead wife
and his living one.

Washing up after supper,
humming the catchiest tune,

you recall the chorus lyrics,
potent with new meaning,

a cipher driving you
to fish the other songs,

one by one, from the shallows
of short-term memory

like lost wedding rings
sluiced down the drain.

You drag them from the S-bend,
rinse them off

and hold them to the light.
How they gleam!

The Woman Who Went Down the Plughole

She'd decided: a new pair of Marigolds,
a bottle of bleach. She'd scrub off the ring
of grime from the walls of the bathtub

if it was the last thing she did. She twirled taps,
watched the stream of water,
laminar as glass, then rougher, faster.

When her phone rang the first time
she let it go. Peeling off a bright glove,
she cleared her throat as it rang again.

No one could say exactly when things changed,
though they had their theories: one neighbour
blamed it on the menopause; another

on the fortune teller at the travelling fair.
Only *she* knew it was that moment
on an ordinary Tuesday, perched on the edge

of a steaming tub. Off she went,
tiny and pale as Fay Wray, arm raised,
not a thing she could do to save herself.

Fortune

Take off your rings. They are clues to your story.

JUDGEMENT

I'm getting a strong signal. You will survive an avalanche. When it comes you'll be prepared. Keep your hand near your face to clear an airspace for your poems. Many suffocate. Make sure you know which way is up. This is the easy part: dribble the spit out from your mouth and see which way it runs. Now dig in the opposite direction.

I see something else coming through: you will give him a kidney. (He's dying, you see, in the physical sense.) Worst-case scenario, temperance — you'll still have to cut back on the Sancerre. Best, a scar and an empty comma on one side of your mid-spine. Each cluster a small lung they stole, breathing life into the glass husk of him until he pinks up. Then he'll ask for the other, the fool . . .

He'll ask you which one you are — in the TV show, I mean: Walt's fallen wife or Hank's — the pretty, bored house-bound mum with the new baby, who knew about the drugs, or the Type-A kleptomaniac sister? Your love will die but oh, you cannot live with another fucking monkey on your back. Mind you heed my forewarning. Honour is nothing. Don't sign anything.

The Moth

If I gave you my life, you would drop it. Wouldn't you?
— Michael Ondaatje, *The English Patient*

In the false darkness of a bar at noon,
his eyes — a clearing in the woods
where something cataclysmic has struck

to let in light like that. You fear
he thinks you're making it all up —
those small coincidences

like that photo of Ford you notice, on the wall,
just after you mention the crush you once had,
or the way you both choose 'Roadhouse Blues'.

You tell him Ford is *even older than him.*
The coin sticks and the jukebox doesn't play
and you see that this story

can only take flight in unspoken thoughts,
imagined and fleeting. A moth flickers
in a shaft of light from the window.

For you it's sweet evanescence,
for him, the full catastrophe.
The vinyl spins, the song begins.

Depth Perception

OCULUS DEXTER

He thanks the cashier as she wraps
twelve truffles in coffee-bean paper,

then hands over a stiff banknote
and all the while he's tapping his foot.

These are his darling's favourite!
He pictures one poised on her lower lip,

her perfect teeth dusted with cocoa,
the pencil tucked in her chignon.

OCULUS SINISTER

He studies the cashier's face as she packs
twelve truffles in tissue and ribbon.

He always pays cash at Josophan's
and doesn't spend long away from the desk.

His sweetheart's smile when she opens the box
and the care she gives to choosing the first

and when she leans to unbutton his shirt
the way the low sun strikes her hair.

OCULUS UTERQUE

The whiskey ice has melted now,
the chocolaterie is closed for the night.

Strewn amid the tissue layers
two truffles, all that remain.

And every surface in the room —
the flocked walls, the brass bed —

is burnished in a purple light,
is burnished in a purple light.

Glass Harp Rhapsody

Is this contentment? he asks, after,
when he's died a little, lost
touch with gravity and sense.
But you're still thinking of the woman
reflected in the mirror-robe you'll never open,
since you have no suitcases,
only the clothes you came in,
now pooled against the wall.

Is this how it feels? Like floating?
But you feel heavy
reflecting on the blurry outline
of her body moving over him;
the curve of her stretch-marked gut;
the *nerve* of her, the small gold pendant
swinging against the delicate bones
of her neck like the holy brown scapular
she wore as an adolescent;
and the note rising in her, rising
as it hasn't since she was nineteen
with her bootlegged Cohen tapes:
obscenity, sex and God.

There's no music in this hotel room,
only this Angelic organ —
wet fingertips traced around
a crystal wineglass rim,
an aria, when it comes,
that seems to last for hours,
silvery and high and strange.

The First Worst Thing

The most intimate thing in the world is not making love
in any of its variations. It's waking in the same bed
as another, stripped of your best jeans, lipstick and blush.

You think you won't sleep, though he sleeps, at last,
on his side, silhouetted by the hotel clock, defined
by an eerie light like a creature from the hadal zone.

It's what you'll recall, for weeks and months to come:
his dark shape, his shoulders so different from your husband's.
Sometime after dawn, despite yourself, you sleep, and then

you wake — dry mouth, mussed hair, your body heat rising,
two eyes on one side of your face, mouth twisted
like a flounder, the bottom feeder you have become.

Fortune Shuffled

TEMPERANCE

Is your wife a fool? you'll ask him, mid-fuck. And the other scenario? An empty life. I see a case of your best Sancerre, coming from cluster to glass. You'll have to give him a pink lung, one side dying. He'll cut up your back, scar your spine in the husk sense. Not physical (comma) worse — something else you'll see through.

Another strong signal from you: this is Space. In which direction is Survive? Be prepared to dig when the air runs out. Will you know which way? I'm getting an avalanche of drivel: Fallen, the opposite of Easy. Face it; you know your part will suffocate many, but each kid's still breathing. See the way your spit comes up clear now? Keep your hand near your mouth.

A warning sign: At 4 a.m. your mind's a monkey house. You cannot live with your sister, the kleptomaniac honey who stole the TV show. She'll waltz in, type you a poem or love you back. Keep mum! Don't heed anything the pretty ask. They are bound to be mean, bored with the new drugs which, on my honour, I knew nothing about. The baby will die in this one. Hanky?

Swimsuit

You pass your phone to your husband
    and ask him, please, to take a picture
of you in your new one-piece, a 1950s style
    with ruched seams your Mum would've loved.

You stand, one foot on hardpacked sand,
    the other in the cool froth of a wavelet,
posing, three-quarter profile, like a starlet,
    tummy pulled in, a sway in your back.

Two small boys tether your hands,
    beaming at their father as he takes the shot.
Retrieving the phone, you double-check
    the photo does the swimsuit justice,

then you thank your husband very much
    and ping the photo off to someone else.

The Ephemerality of Worst Things

The worst thing about worst things:
they're only *worst* until such a time
as you do something that is even

worse, like making love in the back seat of a car,
and not *love*, exactly, and not *a* car but *his*,
since yours has twin booster seats.

Call it impatience, but it happened
at precisely the speed of the world turning, gradual
as Orion, the hunter, easing first one leg

over the low red roofs, next a shoulder,
then the cosmic fire of his nethers,
his famous belt undone.

Does it matter it was Christmas Eve?
Boys in pyjamas, looking for a man in the sky;
you, looking for the sky in a man's eyes,

Orion watching everyone.

Afterwards

When you return to the bistro —
clothed once again in your jeans,
your rifled blouse tucked back in —
and join the chat right where you left off,

a mineral tang persists,
like when, as a child, you put
a copper coin in your mouth, to hide it,
or was it just for sensation's sake?

The tablecloth, stained, strewn
with cracked ponds of crème brûlée,
somebody telling a bawdy joke,
someone else outdoing it.

A platter of Belgian chocolates:
you select a marled snail,
holding it on your tongue
until the other taste dissolves.

You are one side of an abyss.
Everything decent, the other.

The Tale of Lingchi

after an opening line by Ocean Vuong

A happy housewife is all I wanted to be. To pack glass baubles in straw at Michaelmas, to hum as I ironed shirts on Sunday night, to snip and file recipes, cut ham-and-cheese sandwiches into teddy-bear shapes. I never signed up for knife-thrower's assistant.

> *A man walks into a kitchen in his boxers in the small hours for a cup of warm milk because he cannot sleep.*

Yet that's what I became. Cool under fire. Leather-buckled by wrist and ankle to oaken wheel, fixed smile turning up, turning down. No one noticed the half-sadness, the blood that seeped from grazed breast and thigh, or spurted like a string of scarlet scarves pulled from a boy's ear. I was serene. Never sneezed.

> *He smiles — must be sleepwalking — at the sight of the mud-caked form by the sink, jar of pickles in one hand, cheese knife in the other.*

My skin loosened its hold, leaked quarter-formed notions as a torn net leaks minnows. I confided in no one — who'd believe me? The knife-thrower's woman wants for nothing, eats lobster mousseline in a velvet-lined boxcar when the crowds drift from the three-ring.

> *But there's something of his wife's arse in the haunches of this she-beast gorging on Roquefort.*

It was then I became anaemic. My heart startled up, pumped blood and notions faster round my limbs, filled my voice so it cried out with each hit (or miss, depending on your point of view). The crowd squirmed and moved on to burlesque. The tightrope walker caught my eye, with his supple feet and Jesus eyes.

'Why not let the affair blow over? Why leave?'

There was never an affair! Oh, a love affair, perhaps — the kind that people talk about for years, the kind that brings down empires.

Masquerade

When first light gilds the walnut cabinet
and everyone is busy making dreams
or making love you dress silently.
Biting your berry lip, you hold your breath
and slip the silver-plated key inside
the lock. The bow, shaped like a *fleur-de-lis*,
feels cool between your fingertips. You breathe,
the mechanism clicks, and out they slide.
Holding their moulded fabrics to your cheek
(the nacreous pearling of the nautilus,
the moth-wing velveteen), you let your face
decide — obliging handmaid, husband-thief
or succubus, the Whore of Babylon
or plaster saint — which masquerade to don.

Winding Up

OVERTURE

Elbow-to-elbow on the ferry deck:
The wind's up, he says. Your reply
is swallowed by the breeze
and he leans in and asks you to repeat it,

swapping places, saying that his hearing's
shot, knowing that his port side
is a far more handsome presentation.
You do that trick he'll grow to love and tuck

a strand of rain-soaked hair behind your ear.
You wind each other up — like clockwork cars,
or clowns — you twist the keys as tight
as apple skins, then let go.

The thing about winding up —
it can be the start of one journey,
the end of another. A contranym,
or even a conundrum.

FINALE

You meet at the deserted racecourse,
he, pointing out the evening star,
you, counting down the shades of sky —
flamingo, fig, garnet, mussel — the phases

of the setting sun as it subsides
beyond the empty trees, no one
witnessing his mouth on the soft skin
of your collarbone, or throat,

or the starlings' absurd fly-past,
the blown hours eddying like betting slips
along the turf, everything
coming to a standstill at last light.

What would happen if you wound it up,
if it was *wound*, coiled, a hidden injury?
Enduring means both surviving
and suffering — another conundrum.

The Tilted World

Then one day she got up,
her world all out of kilter.
The short trip from bed to kettle
was a skate-park ramp.
   She rapped at her skull
      with her sparkly knuckles
         to reset her balance

but all that week, and the next,
she swerved downhill, to starboard,
as though she were a surfer hanging ten,
as though she were back in Perugia,
   high-heeling cobbled slopes,
      not here, in leafy suburbs,
         shopping for dinner.

It's ear rocks, the grey man said
(he wasn't her first port of call),
canaliths or otoconia to be exact,
(she loved how he knew Greek and Latin!)
   and what rolls in must roll out again.
      And so, he flipped her this way and that —
         on her side, face down, head back —

and sure enough, on the nineteenth try,
      her vertigo was gone.

Night Visit

I woke this morning to a fading scent
of almond flour and lavender,
a sense of something I forgot to do,
some precious chance I'd squandered.

I dreamt of you last night. Among
a baffling mix of guests — the kind that muster
in some half-familiar galley kitchen —
we spoke like any other time, a proper
back-and-forth discussion, and yet I —
ignorant that you were dead —
failed to ask you anything
important, Mother, like, *did you leave*
the salmon out for supper? Or, *should I*
leave my husband? I didn't
hug you when you wiped your hands,
hung your apron up and said
that you had somewhere else to be.

What is a dream but locksmith incognito,
breaking into towers stacked along
the lichened inclines, lonely
as the beehive huts on Skellig Michael.

When you were leaving I was deep in talk
with someone in a wool beret; I only
glanced around and threw a little wave
at your departing figure in the doorway,
wreathed in lilac evening light.

Fortune Reshuffled

THE FOOL

See the way your Mum keeps coming up? She's pretty mean — she'll suffocate you, cut off your breathing with a hank of judgement. Heed your kid sister, the midwife, who's bound to love you. Your baby's fallen for you, honey. He'll waltz you back to the monkey show, give you space to dig. You'll ask him to drizzle Sancerre into your mouth until your split mind clears. (Temperance? No.)

Another warning sign: your honour's the kleptomaniac type that stole the pink from your face. Will the strong drugs put a comma in your near-dying? In this scenario you survive TB. Many know your hand. The husk of a lung is bored from your back; you sense a scar on your spine. Keep it in a glass in case the air runs out.

I'm getting a signal. Something else coming through I knew nothing about: you live in a new house, one you cannot empty of poems. You give each other the best life, a physical side. But don't ask of him. The worst thing: not prepared for any part. Up this way. Easy! And then, clusterfuck from the opposite direction . . . Four die in an avalanche. They're still now.

Witness

If a tree falls in a forest and no one hears, you began,
but didn't finish the thought,
and fear hung between us like smoke,
though we needn't have worried;
the small green car eavesdropping
the whole time we talked,
while outside the weather went through four seasons
and you pointed out dogs that resembled their owners,
and offered me plums from a brown paper bag.
Ask the park bench at Sirius Cove what it knew,
the only proof of a promise—
not in the sense of something sworn,
but something *possible*, like overdue rain.
Beyond the park, that ragged strip of beach
once watched me throw twelve Quicksand roses—
a bouquet too hard to explain—
one by one into the blue.
And probing the shoreline, a thousand lobes
of the harbour must have taken their cue
from your fingers pressing into my mouth
between kisses, the way silence can press into gaps
in an unmanned marriage.

A park bench can be a salvation.
A woman sat next to us one day, to catch her breath,
or out of curiosity.
Please, we have only this hour. But a love affair
must have a witness, and there we'd stayed, next to her,
her bright little dachshund by her feet,
her glasses so thick it's a wonder she could see at all,
though, surely, she could feel
the heat radiate from two strangers,
as another might feel it, years from now,
if they hold their palm to this page.

The Weight of a Marriage

1

There once was a woman who cut her foot
clean off, just to be free
of the jangling charm anklet
she'd fastened to herself, dragging around
its heavy little kettle and cutlery set.
The racket when she turned in her sleep!
She gets about these days on stilts
with rubber tips and no one notices
her bony nib. They look up to her,
through the field glasses of curled-up hands.
It may be painful up there,
but it's so quiet.

2

When she first put it on the marriage felt loose,
a cotton nightdress she'd have to grow into.
She filled her days with busyness,
arranging severed heads
of camellias in crystal bowls, learning
how to make fiddly things — filo pastry,
and babies, which are even more complicated.
A child carries a glass of milk across the room,
treads carefully, spies herself in the glass,
tilts her chin a hair's breadth. The gravity of it:
milk running down her arm
onto her hem and the pretty rug.

3

She learnt that you could keep it light with tricks:
line-drying linens in full sun, neatly folding in
the warmth and, instead of kissing deep,
you could air kiss, the kind that's not a kiss at all —
small engraver of nothing, just another kind of weather,
or a bellwether for the end of something.
A husband's not the only kind to keep a lover
in his arms, another warming on the back boiler
until a swap can be finagled.
There's a rat in the thin space between
a tree and wall, where a girl will crawl
on a quilt of brown pine needles.

4

Picture a man in a low armchair,
leaning over a dismembered newspaper
with all the concentration of a nerve surgeon,
doing the vital work of men, keeping
abreast of all the important things
happening outside in the world.
And a woman at a piano,
picking out a tune, pencilling in the notes
she's forgotten how to read. Her husband
rests his hands lightly on her shoulders
as he passes. She does not look up
but her notes are full of tenderness.

5

When they burst in and slit him open
they found his wife, stone dead, coiled
in his core like a gizzard stone,
diminished, but perfectly formed,
from ring finger to rubber glove.
And there were softened bones of wives of other men
and other women who were the wives of no one.
A heart can bruise like a fruit.
What do you call that colour again
since you don't have *aubergine* Down Under?
Ah, yes, eggplant. Choose carefully:
pick one that feels heavy for its size.

Crystal Anagrams

The most detrimental thing you can do to your crystal is to let it sit alone on the shelf.

CHOOSING

When selecting a stone, or husband, first, keep an open mind and heart. Second, follow your instincts: are you drawn to a particular specimen, one you cannot take your eyes off? Does it pull you in? Despite physical similarities, does one rock/cock jump out at you, become irresistible as the golden sun? Could you pick it among a thousand others — richer, thinner, more successful?

If you're lucky, you won't choose one ending with *-ite*, which could dissolve in your tears. They say you'll feel a jolt when you first touch the special one, like the jump-scare from the citrine stare of your black-footed pussycat, Jasper, who doesn't need you to excite him. (His fragile harness breaks; he doesn't make it back.) A healing bond has formed between you now. Make infinity your new reality. Oh, desire is a light sleeper, manifestly.

To neutralize your stone, smudge with sage near an open upper window, by which I mean the usual: strike a red match, ignite the herb, grasp your stone and move it with intention through the smoke. If it's been a while since your last cleansing — or you feel the stone's holding onto a lot — consider infusing for another thirty seconds.

Condemned

It had been on death row since we'd moved in,
too close to the front of the house,
blocking sun to our daughter's room.
But what finer tree for a garden than a magnolia?
Those three weeks of fondant bloom!
A mistake to prune: it suckered,
sending leggy shoots up like bamboo, ruining
the fractals of its oriental geometry.

Sometimes you must start over.
We sawed through limbs, then trunk,
paid someone to wrestle out the root system.
A pair of stricken lorikeets watched
from the guttering, their home sundered.
We replaced it with a weeping cherry,
the kind that turns back on itself,
never growing any taller.

We did this work together one weekend,
my then-husband and I, the last thing
we collaborated on, apart from
bringing up our children. I miss it all —
the house, the tree, the lorikeets —
especially in late winter, those few weeks
when it almost felt worthwhile.
I'm told there's more light in the house now.

Crystal Anagrams

FEELING

Despite a lack (or lot) of physical similarities you're drawn to another, can't take your eyes off him. A fragile bond has formed between you. Your first husband, J, as per usual, doesn't excite you with his smudged touch. In choosing to be rock he tears a neutral stare from a thousand gasping others. Your second bite of desire scars the heart red, breaks and heals it. Strike back. Make your move. Cock your irresistible pussycat to the new one and hold on!

Citrine, infused with golden light. Cleansed, it harnesses the sun. Oh, special stone, who needs uppers to become richer, thinner, more successful? Manifest! Make your intention a reality. You smoke herb through open windows, feel stoned in thirty seconds. (It's been a while.) When one specimen dissolves — by which I mean ignites — at first you won't feel the jolt.

If selecting a sage you could consider *him* a match. They say you'll pick out one particular ending. Choosing when to jump's the last instinct you follow. Lucky if the stone doesn't pull you with it. Or does it? Could you keep an open mind near the infinity sleepers? Which, since one foot does like jumping, you're among now.

Listening to the Last of the Jonquils

It's terrible to be alone. I don't mean to live alone —
to be be *alone, where no one hears you.*
— Louise Glück, *Averno*

Once you were a door ajar in the hall
of someone's life, which is to say an *option*,
a fake bus stop at a home for the forgetful,
where you wait all day. Your bus doesn't come
and never will. What is deception to the tangled mind?

You think me a mute beauty? My ear trumpets listen
for a shift in season, each corona a roving eye,
witness to the wind's petty thefts:

It was blowing dogs off chains. He had that look he gets
when he takes a yellow pill — suppressed glee
or something — and a crackle in the air,
the metallic rustle of tinsel on a '70s Christmas tree,
the sense of something exciting about to happen.

It galls me, how we pick up only fragments.
I heard the rumours first-hand, right here
at this rotten bench, from Bronze Burner's missus:

It was all a rush; he wore a three-piece,
she, the fake shearling coat of her grandmother's,
a miraculous medal pinned to her blouse.
Her pockets jingled with tiny liquor bottles.
She said they were only for candles.

Remember, remember, to take your pills!
Say *galantamine* — our dying gift.
Pray to us.

When you kill the radio, where do they go — the notes,
in their thirst to be heard, probing the air
with coils of sound? Do they fall
on skin or stone, or cupped ears? Or become
agitated and whine, all those hysterical flutes?

A cabbage white alights on the yolk of a weed head,
long enough to sip nectar
and trade secrets.

The April air bleeds into your lungs,
an aneurism flowers in your head,
a dandelion puff explodes in death,
which means both exhaustion and dispersal.
Shall we wait it out? Endure another year?

Ambiguous Loss

Your child has bitten hers,
and you don't know what to say, to make it right
with the woman who is like a sister to you.

She smiles and says, *We're solid, you and I*,
as though it's inviolable, your holy bond.
And you believe her at the time. You do.

Driving past the kids' old school today,
you saw her in the distance, corralling
her youngest through the gates. You waved.

She might have raised her arm.
It was early and the light was low;
you really couldn't say for sure.

Flare Up

Things fall apart.
— W B Yeats

Things an addict learns to do, silently:
pop two Panadol from a blister pack;
hide a highball in the dishwasher;
pull a cork; empty the recycle bin;
open a tamper-resistant bottle of Ritalin
in your pocket; stream tap water into ice trays;
keep a straight face when a scrap
of glass skewers your bare foot; wipe
a stain from the bathroom floor,
which could be Betadine or dried blood;
lift and lower the lid of a cistern cache;
slide a key in the front-door lock at 3 a.m.
Other things are audible — fierce whispers,
banging doors, all those pretty lies.

Recipe for Redemption

BOLOGNESE

Soak the mince in a cup of full cream milk.[1]
Peel and chop a large brown onion. Cry a little.[2]
Sauté onion in green olive oil over a low heat.[3]
Mash one clove of garlic per child. Add to pan.[4]
Add the softened meat. Pour pink milk down the drain.[5]
Brown the meat until it catches[6] in the pan.
Add crushed tomatoes, herbs, a dash of red wine[7] and a quality stock cube.
Simmer for at least an hour. For best flavour, refrigerate
overnight.[8]

BÉCHAMEL SAUCE

Warm the milk[9] and make a roux with equal parts flour and butter.[10]

---

[1]Milk will soften almost anything.
[2]You're wearing swim goggles but these are different tears.
[3]Don't rush this early stage. Nothing has gone wrong yet.
[4]Children, however, must never be added to pan. This is not a fairy tale.
[5]Think about the sad, glassy eyes of the cattle you saw at the farm-stay last weekend.
[6]This will sound, when stirred, exactly like small waves breaking on a pebble beach you once visited in Sardinia before you were married.
[7]Go on. Have a glass of wine yourself. It's a decent Sangiovese.
[8]You'll now have time to do something for yourself, such as writing, or taking a Valium.
[9]Select your prettiest jug, the one your grandmother gave you.
[10]This is a complicated and delicate process involving careful

Whisk in the milk a little at a time.[11]
Season with salt, pepper and grated nutmeg.[12]

ASSEMBLY, BAKING AND STARTING OVER

Layer the béchamel sauce, Bolognese and lasagna sheets in an oven-proof dish.
Sprinkle liberally with three varieties of grated cheese.[13]
Cover with foil and bake for 40 minutes,[14] removing foil for the last 10.[15] [16]
Soak the mince in a cup of full cream milk.[17]

---

combination of nurturing, reliability and joy. Give it your undivided attention.

[11]A hand whisk is perfectly fine, but an electric whisk in a pastel shade can take years off you.

[12]Nutmeg makes it taste like Christmas. Your children will feel nostalgic and forgive you everything.

[13]Like love, there are as many kinds of cheese as there are hearts.

[14]Have another glass of wine. If you don't finish it off it'll just go to waste.

[15]Neglect to set timer, set off smoke alarm, knock over wine glass, burn fingers, drop Pyrex.

[16]Think about the sad, glassy eyes of your children.

[17]Milk will soften almost anything.

Faith, or a Walking Palm

West of Quito, in the saddle of the Andes,
where air is wreath and mist,
a woman searches among sacred vines.
She's heard the parrots chatter *ayahuasca*,
heard that it can set the spirit loose to wander
unrestrained by trunk and limb,
that it can bend the mind, or make it whole again.

Nothing is fixed; not to say that everything
is broken, or constancy impossible — only
that all of it is mutable.
Nothing abides — neither planetary rings
nor the metal dust that briefly shapes itself
to something vital, then unshapes again.
There is only possibility and a woman
searching botany books in vain,
studying time-lapse photography for proof
a palm tree, resigned to shade,
can work one stilt-root free from darkness
and, like God to Adam,
extend a finger towards light, towards life.

Beneath the canopy a harpy eagle
makes off through gaps in cloud
carrying a sloth like an old carpet,
nerve and sinew clutched in its sleek
claws. To be slow can be fatal,
or it can save you. A tuft
of fluff floats down to feathermoss.
Slow time. Even mountains flatten,
and a palm, given patience, can shift,
infinitesimal as the orbit of a distant planet,
and walk slowly out of the shadows.

Salvage

after U A Fanthorpe

There is a kind of love called *flotsam*.
When winds have paused for breath
where the sea foam eddies,
this love's a shipwrecked plank
proud and quiet on the surface.

And there's a love you could call *jetsam*.
When the hold begins to splinter
and the waterline is rising
it's cast upon the breakers, entrusted to the sea;
washed up, rediscovered as kindling.

Lagan is another kind of love:
When rogue waves have swallowed
the last yellow fingers of the crew,
it drifts from quarter light to where the hagfish lie.
Moored to sunlight, it can always be traced.

And there's a kind of love called *derelict*.
When spite has ripped the spinnakers
and set alight the halyards
this leaden love settles at the heart's pit,
never to be reclaimed.

The Ones We Hurt

All these things swept past us:
a child's first curl, a family crest,
wedding rings — four of them —
a thousand greeting cards
with messages too blurred to read.
There were photos too:
small children on a beach
or blowing out candles on a cake.
Old friends and in-laws floated past,
faces turned away or looking through us
as though at something curious and distant.
There were sudden showers of words
like hail, and silent years between.
We paddled through the churn,
slant rain in our eyes, two people
with a broken oar and tin mug,
waiting for the sky to break.
When the river slowed and widened out
a toy rabbit dangled from the lowest
branches of a drowned tree, and there,
standing on the muddy banks:
the ones we loved, the ones we love still.

The Alchemists

I knew a man who could turn pain into light.
Energy is neither created nor destroyed, he said — an old idea.
Pain is just another kind of energy.

He was the late edit that changed my whole seascape,
like Turner's red buoy, recasting warmth.
I listened, though I'm not a good listener.

We were lying across the bed, better to stargaze,
Permission to Evaporate on repeat, and I told him
Joseph Tawadros plays 52 different instruments.

He told me he'd once hitched a ride from Damascus
with a bust collarbone, a double bass riding shotgun.
The truck driver taught him the trick. I told him

I'd learnt to play oud from Joseph Tawadros:
wearing his bowler, I'd wax the twin arches
of his glorious moustache. We were lying

to each other. I don't play the oud. Never have.
Hats don't suit me; my face is too round!
And I prefer a smooth lip on my, my, *oh my* . . .

What happens in the littoral of pain and light —
a lattice like the white nerves of the sea —
does not translate into poetry.

Outside, fruit bats, the quiet click of rigging.
The cackle of a lone kookaburra —
though he swore it was a monkey.

From the gilt-edged city skyline
light hitched a ride towards us, cleaving pain
from suffering. Dawn is still my medicine.

No matter how I listen now I hear nothing.

Cold Water Swimming in Lyme Regis

And out again, upon the unplumb'd, salt, estranging sea.
— John Fowles, *The French Lieutenant's Woman*

Out again, through the flounce of dulse and tangle,
out again, through the icy bands —

sea fingers clasping calves and thighs,
sea tongues lapping frozen lips.

At twelve degrees the shock can cause your heart
to founder, if you enter suddenly;

it takes a while to grow inured to coldness
though, in less time than you might imagine,

you learn to love the selfishness of being
alone, a different thing to loneliness —

I've heard the mackerel singing in the reach.
I do not doubt that they will sing to me.

In, now — a gasp of breath, the air more savage
than the sea, wind needles, rain needles,

shaft-light sweeping like a search beam
through the swell. It lingers

on the Cobb, a knobbled demi-lune of boulder
pounded by the green fists of the sea.

A man once left me standing on that pier.
He left me there for years. Not really

a man, you understand, but a fiction —
one confected by a real man for his tale.

All that is past. Today these briny spangles
are my diamonds, oarweed my bouquet.

Crystal Anagrams

HEALING

If you're smoking through your thirties — richer, or on your uppers — who keeps the cat? Your first husband, or second? Despite your fragile grasp on reality since, don't consider pussyfooting. You cannot sleep another second. Move out! Oh, choose the more physical one. They say desire's a match you strike near a back window. Stone ignites, forms a thousand bonds. The similarities to the heart are manifest.

Choosing to be open, by holding red Jasper, could make you feel new, infused with light, while harnessed, pulled to need. Its sage intention is to smudge the jolt you'll feel if you become successful, which excites you. You won't dissolve in tears. If you do you'll feel a lot like jumping off a rock.

Sun, and its special citrine touch. Irresistible! The golden cock at first light, early as usual, scaring you from his stone, the last infinity between now and your lucky ending. He doesn't take in your drawn stare, your black mind, which has been neutered of instinct. White hens follow, picking among the thin herbs. Mean eyes of stone. Selecting a particular specimen, one cleans a beak with an open mind. When you jump at one others make for you.

Double-Life Diary

FRIDAY

6 p.m. Arsenic hour.
Nit combs, home-readers, sight-words,
permission-notes, show-and-tells.
Toilet-roll tubes and tape. Sly-replies. Click-to-register.
You will coach their team for the first season,
source satin ribbons in jewel colours
for girl-of-the-game, YouTube the rules.

Later. You will bleach the sink and pots.
Or write a poem. You'll have the second
square of chocolate and a glass of Sancerre,
but abstain from all news and current affairs.
You'll read *The Gift of Dyslexia* and weep,
or *The Captain's Verses* and sigh.
You will dredge Barbie's vacant, smiling head
from a bath half-full of stagnant water.
Pilates tomorrow. Maybe.

SATURDAY

6 a.m. Your bed, a haven for braided limbs
and shiny faces. *Quick, Mum, it's bin day.*
They snuggle in a fug of sleep and lipstick.
Pilates tomorrow, you vow. Definitely.
You plumb the washing basket,
constructing rogue sock balls and tidy piles
of vests and knickers like pancake stacks.

Noon. You bake their favourite cake,
halve the sugar, let them break the eggs.
You'd knit them each a hat — nice for winter

or the glory box — but wool unravels
stitch by stitch, the ball rolls on to undo someone else.

6 p.m. Drop-off time. Duffel bag
with yet more dovetailed socks, labelled shirts
and pinafores for Daddy's House.
Don't forget bunny. Big kiss for Mummy.
In the shower you try to scrub the feeling off,
peel it from your body in long pink scarves.

9 p.m. *Your car*, he says, *it doesn't smell*
like toast today, my love. And your reply,
I'll have to move the car before you ravish me.
We are not paying for parking.

Midnight. A kiss, flung up against the wall
in the tomb-quiet, toy-strewn hall,
the squeak of Barbie's head under your bare heel,
the snap of Lego under his brogue.
Wait! you say, and stuff on one more load
so you can hang it out first thing.

Afterwards. You puzzle your reflection, cloven
by the make-up mirror: two selves
refracted from the bevel — a marled existence.
Pilates tomorrow. Perhaps.

SUNDAY

6 a.m. Exhale. Float right leg to table-top.

Souvenirs of Paradise

Years later, when she thought about her fall,
she'd no regrets — had long outrun those curs —
but guilt's a different beast: a thin scourge,
a parasitic worm no dose of salt
can purge, a cord swung daily to recall
the agony of the innocents,
a fraying hank of rope that penitence
will snap each time she tiptoes off the wall.

She took a crooked highway out of Eden,
forsook the mirror ponds and topiary
for something dark and lovely as a fox den
stocked with ripened fruit. And still she keeps
them in the furthest alcove, almost hidden:
her whip, her haircloth shirt, her thigh cilice.

Redemption, Redleaf Pool

SUNRISE

From his pylon the cormorant watches me
as he once watched Eve in the Garden.
He rents the sky's white silk, holds
his breath longer than I, dives deeper.
He doesn't name the fish, as I do,
doesn't know what he has taught me about God.
When he unpacks his wings in weak sunlight
he looks like an emblem, a fallen angel.

MIDDAY

Gulls, gulls. The graceless calls of them.
Two children take their chances,
spilling from the whispering shade.
They barely make a shadow on the sand.
The younger child inspects a jellyfish,
immortal, but for its errant ways.
The older one impales it with a stick —
this high-tide line is not for sissies.

SUNSET

More fish than I can count
at Redleaf Pool. On the teak pontoon
a woman and a man, barely clad,
practising tai chi;
one squats, the other rises
in waning intervals until, at last, aligned.
Scarlet light fades to lavender.
Renouncing gravity, a pelican lifts off.

Notes from a Room

This beautiful sound. Like you've thrown a plum and an orchard comes back at you.
— Richard Flanagan, *The Narrow Road to the Deep North*

Irina arouses the room.
Deep in the bath, considering
the decline of her flesh, the woman,
giving up on her mortal body, starts to hum
the Bach/Gounod 'Ave Maria' — holy music —
and the room joins in on one low note.

Even walls offer resonance. While every other note
dies off this tone is amplified — it makes the room
vibrate. One rogue tone, and she has conjured music,
as though the bathroom were an orchestra of strings,
as though she'd plucked — when she began to hum —
an instrument, a marble harp. This woman

doesn't care for physics. In the glass she sees a woman
rising from the steam, warbling a note.
Across the tiles, down the stairs, Irina hums,
still dripping. At the old piano in the drawing room
she taps the keys, their hammers ring —
C, C-sharp, D; the walls rebound no music.

That's how it goes: a signal sent out, seeking music,
the off-chance of an echo; it's how a woman
comes to fathom that this far-flung life-ring
for the drowning — this hurtled little note —
is everything. Almost nothing resonates; a room
is just a room, no matter if you hum.

She floats her cargo back upstairs, hummed
inside her head — throat music, sinus music.

Right where she left it is the glassy room:
each feels the other pulse — walls and woman —
strange company, naught in common but this note.
Irina's pale reflection smiles, remembering

the flare of synchrony — like the firing
of a matchbook; hot light, then nothing but the hum
of phosphorous — her story, now, a footnote
in the book of stories. From the street, distant music
drifts through the window, through the ears of a woman
straightening a photo of a bride and groom.

Lowering the window sash, she drowns the music;
where once there was a perfect hum there's just a woman,
and where there lived a holy note, a silent room.

Things Come Together

after a photo by Annie Leibovitz: 'Johnny Cash with his grandson Joseph, Rosanne Cash and June Carter Cash, Hiltons, Virginia, 2001'

It only takes a note, a few lines penned on a card, and the whole thing is salvaged. It might not say much — that's the thing with postcards, you have to work with what little you've got — a dozen words on the back, a thousand in the picture: a man in his rocking chair on a verandah, looking; no, gazing; no, not even gazing; *shining* in the direction of his love, his wife, who, oblivious, holds her autoharp like a child to be soothed, a child who has cut her knee or is overwrought. And there, on guitar, the man's daughter, brow creased in concentration, or mild irritation; next to the man, his grandson — the living proof that it can — or could, at least — all work out.

After Making Love We Play Old Songs

after Galway Kinnell

Our bodies still echoing dregs of ecstasy,
our choices telling our stories: you choose

that track about going home with the waitress,
the way I always do; I choose Dylan,

those mystical lists of his. We puzzle the lyrics,
puzzle how he's been in both our lives

for as long as we can recall, a given, a fixture
like Leonard, or Joni, or Simon & Garfunkel.

We talk about lovers, famous and infamous:
Henry & Anaïs, Edward & Wallis,

and you ask about the Shanghai grip,
if we can try it next time we do this . . .

I say, I always try it, and we laugh so hard
we have to replay the song. Afterwards

we strip the bed, tuck in sheets newly washed
and when my children return it will be as though

this never happened. We never happened
to make a child; we already had plenty between us.

We make a list for the treasure hunt tomorrow
in the garden with your children's children:

beach daisy, pine-cone, magpie-lark,
driftwood, ladybird, Bogon moth,

pink frangipani, Slippery Jack,
crinoline stinkhorn, whip-bird's call.

Milk Beach, Late Summer

Go down to the narrow bay, late afternoon
when light is slant, the harbour a mosaic.
Unfold the cheap table you bought
at the hardware store years ago and set it
so green water laps the rust-flecked legs.
Shake out your whitest table cloth
in the thinning light and lay it out —
a sacred linen in a holy rite;
this is an occasion, as is every dying day.
Unpack a chair apiece. Set out the bread,
some olives, a small bowl for the pits.
Unwrap the cheese, let it ripen.
The water is like foil now, daubed
in steel and mandarin
and here and there the dotted lines
of channel markers on the bay.
The organs of the sky are faint
behind the onionskin of dusk.
Listen out for laughter and the squeak
sand makes beneath bare feet,
and when they come, kiss them on each cheek,
in the European style, and pour them gin,
if you have ice, or if ice is not to hand
pour wine or whiskey. Be glad
they carry nothing but a hand-picked
bunch of herbs tied with kitchen string,
because later, when you nestle
in the flax lilies and spinifex,
your bodies pale and taut as mercury,
you will not wish to be burdened by things.

How You Knew

I wrote to you that ordinary day,
you who had once cracked
your sternum wide apart for me to see

the robin lying on the cage floor,
ribs barely moving, and said to me,
If ever you need my life, come and take it.

You understood it sooner, that's all.
I'd fooled myself for months that this was just
a ruse — a cherub with a quiverful of darts,

folie à deux, a neurochemical trick — or even
vanity, that proud flower bowed over
a looking glass. But this was never just

anything. In a slip of concentration
I wrote: *I didn't love you, then.*
And then a skylight opened for each of us.

The Cut

After I cut your hair, running
the clippers back and forth
until the tiles are littered with tufts
like grey lint swept from the drum
of the tumble-dryer, you pull
your T-shirt off and ask
if I can trim your chest hair. I oblige,
and the whole time you grip
my roving wrist. Next Tuesday
will be one year since they ran
a circular saw up your sternum
and jacked you open,
since they hooked you up
to the heart-lung machine
so they could do their work —
their blessèd work — in a bloodless field.

We circle each other in the kitchen,
old man, middle-aged woman.
If the neighbours spy us through the window,
framed in yellow light, they'd think
we were slow waltzing.
The lightbulb flickers. Careful,
you say, more than once,
and I know your fear is not the catching
in the blades of springy hair —
so different from the smooth locks I've cut
or from the mussel's beard around the base
of your cock — nor of them biting
into pectoral skin, or red-brown nipple.
I've got your heart, I say, and I can feel it,
thumping, thumping, under my left hand
as I shield your chest hair from the whirring.
I can feel it, doing what the heart does.

Contagion

Husbands, too, are scared of me now.
They look at me the way people look

at bloodspots on a handkerchief:
This plague could be the death of us.

See how he tops his gin & tonic up,
see how he pulls his wife away —

and not because she might be tempted
by my charm, but for the germ

that she might catch from me, as though
I were mosquito, airborne droplet, pus.

What starts off as an itch on his wife's wrist
(his smalls no longer have an ironed pleat)

could slowly spread across her limbs and trunk
until she's packed her suitcases and gone.

The woman dies — in art, if not in life,
and all the better if it's savage: haemorrhage,

or pestilence (consumption was a favourite),
we scandal-makers murdered, hanged, or dead

by our own hand: Arsenic! Dagger! Train!
Did those hirsute librettists SET US UP?

Like *concubine*, or *geisha, pan-pan girl* or *whore*
there is no male equivalent to *mistress*, you see.

Tell me, Woman, what would you call yours?
Master? (Surely not — too tricky to distinguish

from your husband!) And *playboy* grants him
far more agency than he deserves.

Oh, I would call mine *drone,* and be his queen,
and buy him rings, and make love all night long

in cheap hotels, and I might have me more than one,
and tell them lies, or tell each one I love him.

Could we at least concoct a kinder end
for Madame Butterfly than hara-kiri?

A day's walk east from Nagasaki is an orchard
robed in stone-fruit trees. There, let her fall;

and let the precious-metal flying beetles
sense the fruit and seek out Cio-Cio-San's

remains, to nourish their white larvae on sweet flesh,
a thousand emerald wings carry her, onwards.

Acknowledgements

Acknowledgements are due to the editors of the following publications where some of these poems, or versions of them, were published first: *Australian Book Review, Australian Poetry Journal, Dreich, F(r)iction, Griffith Review, Howl, The Irish Times, Island, Live Encounters, The London Magazine, Magma, The Moth, Mslexia, Poetry Ireland Review, Poetry London, Poetry News, Rochford Street Review, Southword* and *Washing Windows V*.

'The Moth', 'The Tale of Lingchi' and 'Double-Life Diary', or versions of them, appeared in *Satyress* (Southword Editions, 2020). 'Flare Up' appeared in the collaborative chapbook, *How Bright the Wings Drive Us* (Dreich, 2022). A version of 'Fortune', 'Fortune Shuffled' and 'Fortune Reshuffled' was shortlisted for The Moth Poetry Prize, 2018. 'The Weight of a Marriage' was shortlisted for the Newcastle Poetry Prize and appeared in *The Newcastle Poetry Prize Anthology 2023*. 'Faith, or a Walking Palm' was a finalist for the Montreal International Poetry Prize and appeared in *The Montreal International Poetry Prize Anthology 2024*. 'Notes from a Room' was shortlisted for the 2025 Peter Porter Poetry Prize. 'Cold Water Swimming in Lyme Regis' was runner-up in the 2025 Gwen Harwood Poetry Prize.

Gratitude is due to the Arts Council of Ireland for a Literature Bursary Award that supported the writing of these works, and to the crew at The Gallery Press for their fine work on editing and producing this book. Thanks to *Fallen*'s early readers, especially Daragh Byrne and Alison Gorman. I'm grateful for feedback from the Small Back Room poets, which helped polish many of these poems. Thank you to my children, Grace, Harry and Emily, for their love. And to Graeme, for everything.

Notes

page 12 This poem alludes to 'The Road Not Taken' by Robert Frost and to the children's nursery rhyme 'Ladybird, Ladybird'.

page 18 'the full catastrophe' alludes to a phrase in the 1964 film *Zorba the Greek*.

page 27 The opening line was prompted by the opening line of Ocean Vuong's poem 'Notebook Fragments'.

page 39 Epigraph and several phrases are variations of those found on the following resources:
https://www.magiccrystals.com/pages/healing-crystal-101
https://crystaljoys.com/blogs/the-cj-blog/how-to-care-for-your-crystals

page 49 This poem was prompted by U A Fanthorpe's poem 'Atlas'.

page 51 *Permission to Evaporate* is an album by the Australian multi-instrumentalist and oud virtuoso Joseph Tawadros (self-released, 2014).

page 53 Lines in italics are adapted from T S Eliot's 'The Love Song of J Alfred Prufrock'.

page 63 The title was prompted by Galway Kinnell's poem 'After Making Love We Hear Footsteps'.

page 66 Lines in italics are spoken by the character of Nina in *The Seagull* by Anton Chekhov translated by Elisaveta Fen.